JOURNEY *through* PRAYER

the LIFE of CHRIST

a contemplative prayer journal

belonging to

....

name

....

date

THE LIFE OF CHRIST II: A CONTEMPLATIVE PRAYER JOURNAL

Part of the Journey through Prayer series of journals

Copyright © 2022 by Roseanna M. White

All rights reserved. Reproduction in part or in whole is expressly forbidden without permission from the publisher, with the exception of short snippets for review, promotion, or sharing.

Leukos Puros Journals

13607 Bedford Rd NE
Cumberland, MD 21502

All scripture quotations are taken from the public domain World English Bible. Learn more about this modern English edition based on the 1901 American Standard Version at https://ebible.org/study/

Cover and interior design by Roseanna White Designs, www.RoseannaWhiteDesigns.com
Cover and interior art is by Twins Design Studio via Shutterstock

ISBNs: 979-8-88709-012-2 (paperback)
        979-8-88709-004-7 (hardcover)
        979-8-88709-005-4 (ebook)

What is prayer?

At its most basic level, prayer is communing and communicating with God. How do we do this? By raising our hearts and minds to God. By acknowledging the glory of who He is and seeking to align our will to His. By laying our petitions before Him and asking Him to give us not what we want, but what we need. By listening for His response. By obeying.

How do we pray?

Perhaps you pray best while driving or doing chores, keeping your hands busy. Perhaps you pray best in the quiet of your room. Perhaps you prefer the first minutes of morning, or perhaps you favor the last hour of night.

Or perhaps you like or want to try journaling your prayers, writing down your musings, your contemplations, your requests, and how God has answered. If so, this book is for you!

What is contemplative prayer?

Contemplative prayer is a specific kind of prayer where, instead of either only reciting memorized words or listing your needs for God and then going on your way, you spend time thinking about a theme, Scripture, or idea. As you dwell on the subject, you strive to think about it in ways you haven't before, asking the Lord to show you His truth and lead you closer to Him through the act of contemplation.

What is a prayer journal?

A prayer journal is quite simply a written version of your prayers. It can be a simple notebook, arranged however you please, or something designed specifically for the purpose.

What is this journal and how do I use it?

This journal is designed to guide you through contemplative prayer. The key feature is the guided, focused ideas for themes to ponder each day and space to write your thoughts about them. There are also sections to write down your specific prayer concerns, for your own life or for those who have made a request that you pray for them, and where you can note the Bible verses that have jumped out at you that week in your study.

What makes this journal unique is that it leads you through contemplating the life of Christ and how you can apply it to your own life. In each section you will see:

- ❊ The "announcement" of what the day's contemplation is

- ❊ A classic Christian prayer or song

- ❊ A Scripture passage about the theme

- ❊ A short thought from the journal's author to get you started

- ❊ A list of potential things to consider

- ❊ Space to write your own thoughts

- ❊ A place to note other Scriptures that tie in or which came to mind

- ❊ Space to jot down names and prayer requests to lift before God

You can go through multiple sections a day or take it more slowly. Pray at your own pace, without rushing through the material. Don't feel the need to address all the "Things to Consider" in each section; focus on the one or two that jump out at you, or come up with your own. These lines, these pages are for you. They are between you and the Lord. They are designed to be conducive to thinking deeply, contemplating things you hadn't before, and going deeper in your faith as you seek to learn what God would have for you.

Why are there old prayers included?

You'll see some familiar words and phrases on these pages, meant to remind you of and connect you to not only Christ, but the thousands of years' worth of Christians who have prayed these prayers before you, and who will pray them long after you're gone. Let those old words dwell on your tongue, in your pen, and before your eyes like the sweet gift they are.

This journal series

This journal can be found in several different designs. There are different cover options, and the cover design will echo through the interior design as well. Each section also features new contemplation prompts based on that same "Life of Christ" theme that is used throughout this series. This is to allow you to either choose the cover that appeals to you most or to continue the series after you fill up one volume, for a continued journey of contemplative prayer.

There is a box on the spine for you to write your *own* volume number, and also room on the back to write the dates for easy reference when you want to consult your contemplations later.

Ready for a new prayer journal journey? Check back regularly for the latest Journey through Prayer journal series.

What Bible version is quoted here?

I've chosen to use the only public domain, modern English version of the Bible available: the World English Bible (WEB). Based on the American Standard Version (ASV) from 1901, the World English Bible was updated in the late 20th and early 21st centuries. It uses modern English but relies on a tried-and-true translation. There are both Catholic and Protestant versions of the WEB as well as versions for American, British, and Messianic users specifically.

JESUS IS COMING

Our Father, who art in Heaven,

hallowed be thy name.

Thy kingdom come,

thy will be done

on earth as it is in Heaven.

Give us this day our daily bread

and forgive us our trespasses

as we forgive those who trespass against us.

And lead us not into temptation

but deliver us from evil.

For the kingdom, the power, and the glory

are yours, now and forever.

"Rejoice, you highly favored one! The Lord is with you. Blessed are you among women! ... Behold, you will conceive in your womb and give birth to a son, and shall name him 'Jesus.' He will be great and will be called the Son of the Most High. The Lord God will give him the throne of his father David, and he will reign over the house of Jacob forever. There will be no end to his Kingdom."

Mary said to the angel, "How can this be, seeing I am a virgin?"

The angel answered her, "The Holy Spirit will come on you, and the power of the Most High will overshadow you...."

Mary said, "Behold, the servant of the Lord; let it be done to me according to your word."

~ from Luke 1:28-38
see also Matthew 1:18-25

Mary had plans. She was engaged to be married. She thought she knew what that meant. When the angel of the Lord showed up, everything changed. He declared her highly favored, announced something completely unthinkable…and changed her life forever. Mary could have said no. Instead she said, "Let it be done to me according to your word."

Choose 1 or 2 Things to Consider

* What did it cost Mary to say yes?

* Did she consider what others would say?

* What is God asking you to do today?

* What will it cost you to say yes?

Scriptures and Notes

Prayer Requests

GOOD NEWS
CONFIRMED

Glory be

to the Father,

and to the Son,

and to the Holy Spirit

As it was in the beginning,

is now,

and ever shall be,

world without end.

Amen.

Mary arose in those days and went into the hill country with haste, into a city of Judah, and entered into the house of Zacharias and greeted Elizabeth. When Elizabeth heard Mary's greeting, the baby leaped in her womb; and Elizabeth was filled with the Holy Spirit. She called out with a loud voice and said, "Blessed are you among women, and blessed is the fruit of your womb! Why am I so favored, that the mother of my Lord should come to me? For behold, when the voice of your greeting came into my ears, the baby leaped in my womb for joy! Blessed is she who believed, for there will be a fulfillment of the things which have been spoken to her from the Lord!"

~ Luke 1:39-45

Even when we know God has called us, doubts still plague us; Mary no doubt experienced this as well. As she hurried to her cousin, she probably wondered if the visit from Gabriel had only been a dream. But then, the moment she arrives and calls out a greeting, her much-older cousin confirms the message of the angel! The word Elizabeth uses when she says the babe leapt for joy can mean "frolic." It's the word used for the behavior of a lamb leaping in a pasture. That's the joy that the unborn John experienced when he heard the arrival of the mother of his Savior.

Choose 1 or 2 Things to Consider

- Though most people would have thought Mary's pregnancy was a sin, this godly woman confirmed that it was in fact from the Lord.

- Elizabeth was humbled to be in the presence of the Savior and His mother, even though as Mary's elder and the wife of a priest, she was of a higher station than Mary.

- John, even before he was born, knew total joy at the nearness of the Lord.

- Elizabeth stresses that Mary is blessed because she believed in the impossible.

Scriptures and Notes

Prayer Requests

MAGNIFY THE LORD

O my Jesus,

forgive us our sins,

save us from the fires of hell,

lead all souls to heaven,

especially those who have

most need of your mercy.

Mary said,

"My soul magnifies the Lord.

My spirit has rejoiced in God my Savior,

for he has looked at the humble state of his servant.

For behold, from now on, all generations will call me blessed.

For he who is mighty has done great things for me.

Holy is his name.

His mercy is for generations and generations on those who fear him.

He has shown strength with his arm.

He has scattered the proud in the imagination of their hearts.

He has put down princes from their thrones,

and has exalted the lowly.

He has filled the hungry with good things.

He has sent the rich away empty.

He has given help to Israel, his servant, that he might remember mercy,

as he spoke to our fathers,

to Abraham and his offspring forever."

~ Luke 1:46-55

This passage of praise from Mary is traditionally called "The Canticle of Mary" or "The Magnificat," which means "an utterance of praise." In this beautiful song, Mary not only thanks God for what He is doing for her and through her, she praises Him for being who He is—a God who is merciful, who provides for His children, who loves them, who sends help, who is mighty and faithful.

Choose 1 or 2 Things to Consider

❀ All of Mary's joy is directed to the mighty, holy God.

❀ Mary looks back to history and recalls all that God has done through the generations.

❀ God so often works His wonders by upsetting the natural order.

❀ When we are hungry, God fills us.

Scriptures and Notes

Prayer Requests

JESUS IS HERE

Hurry, God,

to deliver me.

Come quickly

to help me, Lord.

~ Psalm 70:1

While they were there, the day had come for her to give birth. She gave birth to her firstborn son. She wrapped him in bands of cloth and laid him in a feeding trough, because there was no room for them in the inn.

~ Luke 2:6-7
see also Matthew 2

Were man to write the story of the greatest King to ever live, we perhaps would have had Him born into the most beautiful palace ever built, with fanfare and hype. Instead, the Lord of all Creation made a quiet debut in a small town, where His parents hadn't even been able to secure a proper guest room. His crib was an animal trough. But His circumstances could not change who He is.

Choose 1 or 2 Things to Consider

- ❀ "Firstborn" indicates not just birth order among multiple children, but inheritance. The firstborn son always received a double portion, which he was to use to care for his mother after his father's death.

- ❀ How do you think Joseph's family received them?

- ❀ What must it have been like to give birth to a child you knew was so precious in such humble circumstances?

- ❀ Why do you think God chose to have His Son be born in this situation?

Scriptures and Notes

Prayer Requests

BEHOLD, THE CHILD

Lord, make me an instrument of your peace.
Where there is hatred, let me bring love;
where there is injury, pardon;
where there is doubt, faith;
where there is despair, hope;
where there is darkness, light;
where there is sadness, joy.
O Divine Master, grant that I may not
so much seek to be consoled as to console,
to be understood as to understand,
to be loved as to love.
For it is in giving that we receive,
it is in pardoning that we are pardoned,
and it is in dying
that we are born to eternal life.

Behold, there was a man in Jerusalem whose name was Simeon. This man was righteous and devout, looking for the consolation of Israel, and the Holy Spirit was on him. He came in the Spirit into the temple. When the parents brought in the child, Jesus, then he received him into his arms and blessed God, and said,

"Now you are releasing your servant, Master,

according to your word, in peace;

for my eyes have seen your salvation,

which you have prepared before the face of all peoples;

a light for revelation to the nations,

and the glory of your people Israel."

Joseph and his mother were marveling at the things which were spoken concerning him. Simeon blessed them, and said to Mary, his mother, "Behold, this child is appointed for the falling and the rising of many in Israel, and for a sign which is spoken against. Yes, a sword will pierce through your own soul, that the thoughts of many hearts may be revealed."

~ *from* Luke 2:22-38

As Mary and Joseph obeyed the commands given to Israel for purification and presentation of each firstborn son to Him, He had a special arrangement made for them. Not one but two elders greeted them at the temple with wisdom, knowledge, and prophecy. Jesus would have been behaving like all babies do—nursing, crying, making a mess of his diaper, sleeping, cuddling, cooing. But God met these specially chosen parents with a reminder of how *not* normal their baby was.

Choose 1 or 2 Things to Consider

❀ Sometimes we can know that God intends great things without knowing the details of what it will involve.

❀ Anna is another faithful prophet, sent by God to arrive at that very hour so that she could behold the infant Lord.

❀ Are we listening for God's whisper about when we should meet Him?

❀ Are we offering wisdom and the words of the Lord to those who are seeking Him?

Date

Scriptures and Notes

Prayer Requests

IN HIS FATHER'S HOUSE

Bless us, O Lord,
and these thy gifts,
which we are about to receive
from thy bounty,
through Christ our Lord.
Amen.

The child was growing, and was becoming strong in spirit, being filled with wisdom, and the grace of God was upon him.

When he was twelve years old, they went up to Jerusalem according to the custom of the feast; and when they had fulfilled the days, as they were returning, the boy Jesus stayed behind in Jerusalem. When they didn't find him, they returned to Jerusalem, looking for him. After three days they found him in the temple, sitting in the middle of the teachers, both listening to them and asking them questions. All who heard him were amazed at his understanding and his answers. When they saw him, they were astonished; and his mother said to him, "Son, why have you treated us this way? Behold, your father and I were anxiously looking for you."

He said to them, "Why were you looking for me? Didn't you know that I must be in my Father's house?" They didn't understand the saying which he spoke to them. And he went down with them and came to Nazareth. He was subject to them, and his mother kept all these sayings in her heart.

~ from Luke 2:40-52

*M*ary and Joseph must have been frantic when they realized Jesus wasn't with the other children in their group of travelers! They hurried back to Jerusalem to find Him, but it took three agonizing days before they did. Jesus clearly did not mean to cause them suffering, though He did—we know, however, that it was no sin for Him to do so. Even so, He returned with them and was obedient to them, subjecting Himself to their authority.

Choose 1 or 2 Things to Consider

❀ Jesus demonstrated to them that He knew He was and needed to be, but he nevertheless submitted to their parental guidance for several more years.

❀ The holy parents must have been reminded anew of how unique and special this Child of theirs was, and the burden that placed on them to raise Him well.

❀ The wisest men of the age marveled at the insights of a child.

❀ Jesus, a true child prodigy in matters of faith, went on to use children as His examples of truest faith many times in the Gospels.

 Date _______________

Scriptures and Notes

Prayer Requests

JESUS IS BAPTIZED

In the name of the Father

and of the Son

and of the Holy Spirit.

Amen.

Then Jesus came from Galilee to the Jordan to John, to be baptized by him. But John would have hindered him, saying, "I need to be baptized by you, and you come to me?"

But Jesus, answering, said to him, "Allow it now, for this is the fitting way for us to fulfill all righteousness." Then he allowed him.

Jesus, when he was baptized, went up directly from the water: and behold, the heavens were opened to him. He saw the Spirit of God descending as a dove, and coming on him. Behold, a voice out of the heavens said, "This is my beloved Son, with whom I am well pleased."

~ Matthew 3:13-16

see also Mark 1; Luke 3; John 1

Though in many cases the four Gospels focus on different stories or interpretations of the stories, this monumental event is recorded almost identically in all of them. Clearly all the writers agreed that it was critical that we know the moment at which the Holy Spirit descended upon Christ, and that it was only after this that He began His ministry, despite being filled with God's wisdom from childhood on.

Choose 1 or 2 Things to Consider

❀ Jesus later tells Nicodemus that in order to be born again, we must "be born of water and the Spirit," indicating the importance of baptism.

❀ As John baptized, he proclaimed that the Kingdom of God was near at hand.

❀ When Christ began preaching, He proclaimed that the Kingdom of God was *here*.

❀ Why did this act of baptism please God the Father?

Date _______________________

Scriptures and Notes

Prayer Requests

WATER TO WINE AT A WEDDING

O Lord God,
I love you above all things
and I love my neighbor
for your sake
because you are the highest,
infinite and perfect good,
worthy of all my love.
In this love
I intend to live and die.
Amen.

There was a wedding in Cana of Galilee. Jesus' mother was there. Jesus also was invited, with his disciples, to the wedding. When the wine ran out, Jesus' mother said to him, "They have no wine."

Jesus said to her, "Woman, what does that have to do with you and me? My hour has not yet come."

His mother said to the servants, "Whatever he says to you, do it."

Now there were six water pots of stone, containing twenty to thirty gallons apiece. Jesus said to them, "Fill the water pots with water." So they filled them up to the brim. He said to them, "Now draw some out, and take it to the ruler of the feast." So they took it. When the ruler of the feast tasted the water now become wine, and didn't know where it came from (but the servants who had drawn the water knew), the ruler of the feast called the bridegroom and said to him, "Everyone serves the good wine first, and when the guests have drunk freely, then that which is worse. You have kept the good wine until now!"

~ from John 2:1-11

Though Jesus says it isn't yet time for Him to work, He nevertheless respects and obeys His mother's request to help this family in a moment when they needed it. Jesus listened to an earnest petition, and also performed His first miracle at an event that celebrated the creation of a new family through marriage.

Choose 1 or 2 Things to Consider

❀ Jesus never touches the water or blesses it; it is the obedient action of the servants that demonstrates the miracle.

❀ When Jesus acts, it is to produce the best thing.

❀ Marriage is blessed in this action and goes on to feature in many of Jesus's parables.

❀ Do you think this couple knew what had happened?

Date ___________________

Scriptures and Notes

Prayer Requests

THE BLESSED AND THE KINGDOM OF HEAVEN

Lord, by the light of the Holy Spirit
you have taught the hearts of your faithful.
In the same Spirit
help us to relish what is right
and always rejoice in your consolation.

"Blessed are the poor in spirit,
for theirs is the Kingdom of Heaven.
Blessed are those who mourn,
for they shall be comforted.
Blessed are the gentle,
for they shall inherit the earth.
Blessed are those who hunger and thirst for righteousness,
for they shall be filled.
Blessed are the merciful,
for they shall obtain mercy.
Blessed are the pure in heart,
for they shall see God.
Blessed are the peacemakers,
for they shall be called children of God.
Blessed are those who have been persecuted for righteousness' sake,
for theirs is the Kingdom of Heaven.
"Blessed are you when people reproach you, persecute you, and say
    all kinds of evil against you falsely, for my sake. Rejoice, and be
    exceedingly glad, for great is your reward in heaven. For that is
    how they persecuted the prophets who were before you.

~ Matthew 5:3-12
see also Luke 6:20-49

In these familiar Beatitudes, Jesus yet again upsets the natural order and redefines "the blessed" as they're seen through the eyes of God. Man says, "Blessed are the rich, the powerful, the strong." But the Lord teaches us that when we are weak, God will provide strength far beyond what we could achieve on our own.

Choose 1 or 2 Things to Consider

❀ Would people describe you as gentle?

❀ What does it mean to "inherit the earth"?

❀ Do you hunger and thirst for righteousness?

❀ Where do you long to receive mercy, and how can you give it?

Scriptures and Notes

Prayer Requests

THE TRANSFIGURATION

Father,
I abandon myself into your hands;
do with me what you will.
Whatever you may do, I thank you:
I am ready for all, I accept all.
Let only your will be done in me,
and in all your creatures –
I wish no more than this, O Lord.
Into your hands I commend my soul:
I offer it to you with all the love of my heart,
for I love you, Lord, and so need to give myself,
to surrender myself into your hands without reserve,
and with boundless confidence,
for you are my Father.

After six days, Jesus took with him Peter, James, and John his brother, and brought them up into a high mountain by themselves. He was changed before them. His face shone like the sun, and his garments became as white as the light. Behold, Moses and Elijah appeared to them talking with him.

Peter answered and said to Jesus, "Lord, it is good for us to be here. If you want, let's make three tents here: one for you, one for Moses, and one for Elijah."

While he was still speaking, behold, a bright cloud overshadowed them. Behold, a voice came out of the cloud, saying, "This is my beloved Son, in whom I am well pleased. Listen to him."

When the disciples heard it, they fell on their faces, and were very afraid. Jesus came and touched them and said, "Get up, and don't be afraid." Lifting up their eyes, they saw no one, except Jesus alone.

~ Matthew 17:1-8

see also Mark 9:2-13; Luke 9:28-36

In this second event in which the voice of God the Father proclaims Jesus to be His Son, in whom He is well-pleased, He adds a command: *Listen to Him.* The disciples who witnessed this miraculous event could only respond in one way: to fall on their faces before the glory of God, not only in awe but in fear…fear which Jesus banishes with a touch and calm assurance.

Choose 1 or 2 Things to Consider

❀ Does the word of the Lord ever leave you fearful?

❀ Other Gospels mention that the disciples were half asleep when they startled awake to witness the events.

❀ Peter wanted to stay there on the mount—why?

❀ Peter's idea (other Gospels specify that he didn't know what else to say) is interrupted by God's voice.

Scriptures and Notes

Prayer Requests

TRUE COMMUNION

Soul of Christ, sanctify me;
body of Christ, save me;
blood of Christ, inebriate me;
water from the side of Christ, wash me;
passion of Christ, strengthen me.
O good Jesus, hear me;
within your wounds hide me;
suffer me not to be separated from you;
from the malicious enemy defend me;
in the hour of my death call me,
and bid me come to you
that with your saints I may praise you
forever and ever. Amen.

He said to them, "I have earnestly desired to eat this Passover with you before I suffer, for I tell you, I will no longer by any means eat of it until it is fulfilled in God's Kingdom." He received a cup, and when he had given thanks, he said, "Take this and share it among yourselves, for I tell you, I will not drink at all again from the fruit of the vine, until God's Kingdom comes."

He took bread, and when he had given thanks, he broke and gave it to them, saying, "This is my body which is given for you. Do this in memory of me." Likewise, he took the cup after supper, saying, "This cup is the new covenant in my blood, which is poured out for you.

~ Luke 22:15-20

see also Matthew 26:17-29; Mark 14:12-25

Many Christians call the breaking of bread and sharing of the cup *communion*, because it allows us to come into full communion with God through Christ. It's also called *the Eucharist*, which means "thanksgiving," because we are so grateful for the privilege of partaking of the saving flesh and blood of Christ.

Choose 1 or 2 Things to Consider

❀ We are called to participate likewise in this act of communion.

❀ Read John 6:41-71. In this passage, Jesus makes it clear that "eating His flesh" is not optional. Do we try to make this "hard teaching" too easy?

❀ The Third Cup in the Passover meal is called the Cup of Blessing and is the one that Christ declared to be His blood, showing us that He is blessing all who partake.

❀ They leave the meal prematurely after this Third Cup, before sharing the Fourth Cup, which is the Cup of Salvation.

Scriptures and Notes

Prayer Requests

A GARDEN OF AGONY

Let nothing disturb you,
Let nothing frighten you,
All things are passing away:
God never changes.
Patience obtains all things
Whoever has God lacks nothing;
God alone suffices.

He knelt down and prayed, saying, "Father, if you are willing, remove this cup from me. Nevertheless, not my will, but yours, be done."

An angel from heaven appeared to him, strengthening him. Being in agony, he prayed more earnestly. His sweat became like great drops of blood falling down on the ground.

When he rose up from his prayer, he came to the disciples and found them sleeping because of grief, and said to them, "Why do you sleep? Rise and pray that you may not enter into temptation."

While he was still speaking, a crowd appeared, Judas leading them. He came near to Jesus to kiss him.

When those who were around him saw what was about to happen, they said to him, "Lord, shall we strike with the sword?" A certain one of them struck the servant of the high priest, and cut off his right ear.

But Jesus answered, "Let me at least do this"—and he touched his ear and healed him.

~ from Luke 22:39-51

see also Matthew 26:36-46; Mark 14:32-42; John 18:1

esus's prayer in the garden is one of the most moving examples of His great love for mankind. We see His dread—of death, or of the shadow of sin He is about to receive that will separate Him, for the first time, from the Father?—manifesting itself in the deepest agony. But even in that moment, He chooses God's will, acts in love, and even offers healing to His enemies.

Choose 1 or 2 Things to Consider

❀ Jesus, in His human will, did not *want* to go through the coming ordeal—but He submitted to the will of the Father.

❀ What must all the sins of history have looked like to the sinless eyes of Christ before they settled upon Him?

❀ In this hour of deepest torment, an angel—a messenger of God—appeared not to offer wisdom but to give comfort.

❀ How can we minister in comfort to those going through trials?

Scriptures and Notes

Prayer Requests

JESUS IS SCOURGED

Walk in the light,
the beautiful light.
Come where the dewdrops
of mercy shine bright.
Shine all around us
by day and by night.
Jesus, the light of the world.

"Which of the two do you want me to release to you?"

They said, "Barabbas!"

So when Pilate saw that nothing was being gained, but rather that a disturbance was starting, he took water and washed his hands before the multitude, saying, "I am innocent of the blood of this righteous person. You see to it."

All the people answered, "May his blood be on us and on our children!"

Then he released Barabbas to them, but Jesus he flogged and delivered to be crucified.

~ *from* Matthew 27:19-26

see also Mark 15:15; Luke 23:25; John 19:1-3

The Roman scourge was a multi-strand whip with metal balls, bones, and spikes attached to it, to rip the flesh from the victim. Why would Pilate have turned Jesus over for scourging when he thought Him innocent? Some ancient traditions say he was hoping that seeing one of their own abused by Roman "justice" would move the crowds to pity and help them see Him as one of them.

Choose 1 or 2 Things to Consider

❀ Does the water Pilate washed his hands with provide for his innocence like a sort of baptism?

❀ The people cry out for Jesus's blood to be upon them and their children, in affect taking the guilt of His death upon their generations.

❀ Jesus's blood *has* been upon us all—but it is cleansing and saving instead of condemning.

❀ Jesus underwent this horrific torture willingly for us.

Scriptures and Notes

Prayer Requests

KING OF THE CURSE

O my God,
I love Thee above all things,
with my whole heart and soul,
because Thou art all good
and worthy of all love.
I love my neighbor as myself
for the love of Thee.
I forgive all who
have injured me,
and ask pardon of all
whom I have injured.

Then the governor's soldiers took Jesus into the Praetorium, and gathered the whole garrison together against him. They stripped him and put a scarlet robe on him. They braided a crown of thorns and put it on his head, and a reed in his right hand; and they kneeled down before him and mocked him, saying, "Hail, King of the Jews!" They spat on him, and took the reed and struck him on the head. When they had mocked him, they took the robe off him, and put his clothes on him, and led him away to crucify him.

~ Matthew 27:27-31

see also Mark 15:17; John 19:2-5

Thorns are a direct result of the curse in the Garden of Eden, a consequence of our sin; it is with this very physical reminder of all that is wrong with humanity that the King of all was crowned. What the Roman soldiers used as mockery, however, Jesus accepted in humility as truth. He knew that He was being crowned with our sins so that He could defeat them, defeat death, and restore the true crown of glory to us all in heaven.

Choose 1 or 2 Things to Consider

❀ Mockery and ridicule are always a risk when one is a follower of Jesus.

❀ When we say we follow Jesus but don't live it out in our actions, we are shoving that crown of thorns onto His head.

❀ Does Christ truly reign in our hearts?

❀ Adam was the first prince of the earth, punished by thorns for disobedience; Jesus is the true prince of heaven and earth, crowned with the curse but defeating it.

Date _______________________

Scriptures and Notes

Prayer Requests

CARRYING HIS CROSS

We adore you, O Christ,

and we praise you,

because by your holy Cross

you have redeemed the world.

When they had mocked him, they took the robe off him, and put his clothes on him, and led him away to crucify him.

As they came out, they found a man of Cyrene, Simon by name, and they compelled him to go with them, that he might carry his cross.

~ Matthew 27:31-32
see also Mark 15:21; Luke 23:26; John 19:17

The verses are short, but how long the road must have been for Jesus! Already exhausted from a sleepless, stressful night, weakened from the scourging, now bearing His own horrible means of death outside the city, Jesus reached the end of His physical abilities. He did not ask for help, but a man was compelled to come to his assistance. Traditionally, His journey is called the *Via Dolorosa* or "Road of Sorrow."

Choose 1 or 2 Things to Consider

* Jesus's cross was for a purpose—the salvation of us all.

* What is the purpose of your burdens?

* When Jesus tells us to take up our cross, He means not only our burdens, but our purposes and callings.

* Jesus bore the cross without objecting to His innocence, because He carried it for us, the guilty.

Scriptures and Notes

Prayer Requests

THE CRUCIFIXION

My God, my God, why have you forsaken me?
Why are you so far from helping me,
and from the words of my groaning?
~ Psalm 22:1

He went out, bearing his cross, to the place called "The Place of a Skull", which is called in Hebrew, "Golgotha", where they crucified him, and with him two others, on either side one, and Jesus in the middle…

But standing by Jesus' cross were his mother, his mother's sister, Mary the wife of Clopas, and Mary Magdalene. Therefore when Jesus saw his mother, and the disciple whom he loved standing there, he said to his mother, "Woman, behold, your son!" Then he said to the disciple, "Behold, your mother!" From that hour, the disciple took her to his own home.

After this, Jesus, seeing that all things were now finished, that the Scripture might be fulfilled, said, "I am thirsty!" Now a vessel full of vinegar was set there; so they put a sponge full of the vinegar on hyssop, and held it at his mouth. When Jesus therefore had received the vinegar, he said, "It is finished!" Then he bowed his head and gave up his spirit.

~ from John 19:17, 25-30
see also Matthew 27:27-44; Mark 15:16-32; Luke 23:33-46

$\mathcal{E}$ ach of the Gospel accounts highlights different things that Jesus said in His last moments; what every early believer understood but which we today may not is that each word He spoke would have cost Him strength and caused Him great agony. He would have had to put His weight on His pierced feet to push Himself up enough to draw in a deep breath and to give these final words.

Choose 1 or 2 Things to Consider

❀ Do we ever turn away from trials instead of facing loss and risking danger?

❀ The women who had followed Him faithfully were following Him still.

❀ What choice can you make today to remain faithful even when it's difficult or frightening?

❀ Matthew records Jesus crying out, "My God, my God, why have you forsaken me?" from the cross.

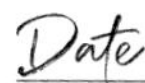

Scriptures and Notes

Prayer Requests

HE IS RISEN!

He is risen!

He is risen indeed!

Alleluia! Alleluia!

Now after the Sabbath, as it began to dawn on the first day of the week, Mary Magdalene and the other Mary came to see the tomb. Behold, there was a great earthquake, for an angel of the Lord descended from the sky and came and rolled away the stone from the door and sat on it. For fear of him, the guards shook, and became like dead men. The angel answered the women, "Don't be afraid, for I know that you seek Jesus, who has been crucified. He is not here, for he has risen, just like he said. Go quickly and tell his disciples, 'He has risen from the dead, and behold, he goes before you into Galilee; there you will see him.'"

They departed quickly from the tomb with fear and great joy, and ran to bring his disciples word. As they went to tell his disciples, behold, Jesus met them, saying, "Rejoice!"

They came and took hold of his feet, and worshiped him.

~ from Matthew 28:1-10

see also Mark 16:1-13; Luke 24:1-12 ; John 20:1-25

These dedicated women wanted to give the body of their Master the honor and respect they felt He was due…but they made one mistake: they were seeking the living among the dead! Their devotion, however, still earned them the most precious of all commands. They had the honor of being the first to receive and share the news of the Lord's resurrection.

Choose 1 or 2 Things to Consider

❀ Does the thought of Jesus's resurrection make you so joyful that you run to tell others?

❀ The soldiers at the tomb saw everything that happened but were, as Matthew says, "like stone."

❀ Do you know anyone who is "like stone" in the face of the news of the risen Lord?

❀ Has your heart grown hard to this miracle that we sometimes take for granted?

Scriptures and Notes

Prayer Requests

THE ASCENSION

God, our loving Father,
you sent your Son,
Jesus Christ, into this world
to counter all the forces of evil, sin,
suffering and death,
and to overcome evil with the force of good;
hatred with the power of love,
your great love for us in Jesus.
Help us never to curse the darkness,
but to join with you in bringing
Your light into this world.

Therefore, when they had come together, they asked him, "Lord, are you now restoring the kingdom to Israel?"

He said to them, "It isn't for you to know times or seasons which the Father has set within his own authority. But you will receive power when the Holy Spirit has come upon you. You will be witnesses to me in Jerusalem, in all Judea and Samaria, and to the uttermost parts of the earth."

When he had said these things, as they were looking, he was taken up, and a cloud received him out of their sight. While they were looking steadfastly into the sky as he went, behold, two men stood by them in white clothing, who also said, "You men of Galilee, why do you stand looking into the sky? This Jesus, who was received up from you into the sky, will come back in the same way as you saw him going into the sky."

~ Acts 1:6-11

see also Mark 16:19

*E*ven after His death and resurrection, Jesus's disciples can't quite wrap their heads around the fact that His Kingdom is not of the earth. But after this, they never question it again—He made their mission clear and then left them to it by departing miraculously from their sight. We can well imagine them just staring up at the sky, but we don't need to. We know He'll return.

Choose 1 or 2 Things to Consider

- Jesus yet again answers the question they should have been asking instead of the question they did.

- Have you ever received an answer to the prayers you should have been praying instead of the ones you were?

- How can we train ourselves to ask the right questions?

- Do you ever feel like you're staring at the sky, waiting?

Date

Scriptures and Notes

Prayer Requests

THE HOLY SPIRIT DESCENDS

Come, Holy Spirit,
fill the hearts of your faithful.
And kindle in them the fire of your love.
Send forth your Spirit
and they shall be created.
And you will renew
the face of the earth.

Now when the day of Pentecost had come, they were all with one accord in one place. Suddenly there came from the sky a sound like the rushing of a mighty wind, and it filled all the house where they were sitting. Tongues like fire appeared and were distributed to them, and one sat on each of them. They were all filled with the Holy Spirit and began to speak with other languages, as the Spirit gave them the ability to speak.

~ Acts 2:1-4

From the moment they receive the Holy Spirit, we see the disciples behaving very differently. No longer are they bickering about who's the greatest or wondering about politics. Once filled with the Spirit, they boldly walk out their mission. Even though in Acts we see they are still flawed and human, we also see that they act in the authority of Christ, being filled with the same Spirit that had descended on Him.

Choose 1 or 2 Things to Consider

- ❀ Jesus promised this Comforter and Teacher because He knew we would need the connection and assurance.

- ❀ The Spirit is depicted as a dove, as wind, and as fire—which speaks most to you?

- ❀ Not only did the Spirit enable the disciples to speak in other languages, He also enabled the crowds to hear in their native languages.

- ❀ The Holy Spirit enabled Christ to work His mission and enables us to work ours.

Scriptures and Notes

Prayer Requests

THE HEAVENLY VIEW

God, in Baptism
you called me by name
and made me a member
of your people, the Church.
Help all your people
to know their vocation in life,
and to respond by living
a life of holiness.

A great sign was seen in heaven: a woman clothed with the sun, and the moon under her feet, and on her head a crown of twelve stars. She was with child. She cried out in pain, laboring to give birth.

Another sign was seen in heaven. Behold, a great red dragon, having seven heads and ten horns, and on his heads seven crowns. His tail drew one third of the stars of the sky, and threw them to the earth. The dragon stood before the woman who was about to give birth, so that when she gave birth he might devour her child. She gave birth to a son, a male child, who is to rule all the nations with a rod of iron. Her child was caught up to God and to his throne. The woman fled into the wilderness, where she has a place prepared by God, that there they may nourish her one thousand two hundred sixty days.

~ Revelation 12:1-6

In the Gospels, we get the facts of Christ's birth from our earthly perspective. In Revelation, we are given a new view of the event from the heavenly, spiritual perspective. This perspective shows us the war waged in a realm beyond our eyes...a war still raging.

Choose 1 or 2 Things to Consider

- This section, where we see Mary giving birth to Christ, crowned with stars, is why tradition calls her the Queen (Mother) of Heaven.

- How often do you consider the heavenly implications of your earthly actions and experiences?

- Are you mindful of the spiritual side of "everyday" events?

- How can you take a heavenly perspective on other events in history?

Date

Scriptures and Notes

Prayer Requests

CHRIST REIGNS

Eternal Word,

only begotten Son of God,

teach me true generosity.

teach me to serve you as you deserve,

to give without counting the cost,

to fight heedless of wounds,

to labor without seeking rest,

to sacrifice myself

without thought of any reward

save the knowledge

that I have done your will.

Amen.

And among the lamp stands was one like a son of man, clothed with a robe reaching down to his feet, and with a golden sash around his chest. His head and his hair were white as white wool, like snow. His eyes were like a flame of fire. His feet were like burnished brass, as if it had been refined in a furnace. His voice was like the voice of many waters. He had seven stars in his right hand. Out of his mouth proceeded a sharp two-edged sword. His face was like the sun shining at its brightest. When I saw him, I fell at his feet like a dead man.

He laid his right hand on me, saying, "Don't be afraid. I am the first and the last, and the Living one. I was dead, and behold, I am alive forever and ever. Amen."

~ Revelation 1:13-18

In the end of the Gospels and the beginning of Acts, we see Christ ascending into Heaven, to sit at the Father's right hand. Through John's revelation, we get a glimpse of Him is His glory, not only ruling the heavenly realms, but ruling all of creation. Yet from His throne, He is still concerned first and foremost with His Church.

Choose 1 or 2 Things to Consider

❀ The problems, strengths, and weaknesses of those churches represent us all.

❀ What faults do you see in the worldwide Church today?

❀ How can you promote healing and strength and unification in the Church?

❀ Consider writing a letter to a nearby church to offer encouragement.

Date

Scriptures and Notes

Prayer Requests

Repeat the Cycle

One of the beautiful things about contemplative prayer is what happens when we repeat the same material. What jumped out at you this time will now be the foundation you're standing on when you go through the material again. New questions or thoughts or ideas will demand your attention when you read through the same passages next time.

With this in mind, these journals are created to be repeated. You'll find several different designs in the same series; the interior material will be largely the same, only with new prompts for writing. The cover and design will change as well, to differentiate them on your shelf or in your drawer. They're each designed with space to write your own numbering system and date span on the spine and back cover for easy reference. Repeat the series as many times as you desire!

Ready for a new series? Check back regularly for the latest Journey through Prayer designs. Your suggestions for studies and topics you'd like to see are always welcome. Email me at roseanna@roseannawhite.com to share your ideas.